THE CLASSICAL FARM

PETER DIDSBURY

THE CLASSICAL
FARM

BLOODAXE BOOKS

ISBN: 1 85224 012 1

First published 1987 by
Bloodaxe Books Ltd,
P.O. Box 1SN,
Newcastle upon Tyne NE99 1SN.

Bloodaxe Books Ltd acknowledges
the financial assistance of Northern Arts.

Typesetting by Bryan Williamson, Manchester.

Cover printing by
Tyneside Free Press Workshop Ltd, Newcastle upon Tyne.

Printed in Great Britain by
Biddles Limited, Guildford, Surrey.

For Sarah, David and Sam

Acknowledgements

Acknowledgements are due to the editors of the following publications in which some of these poems first appeared: *Bête Noire, Helix, The Literary Review, Quarto, Slightly Soiled, Smoke, The Times Literary Supplement, To Build a Bridge* (Lincolnshire & Humberside Arts, 1982), and *Verse*.

Six poems from this collection appeared in Douglas Dunn's anthology *A Rumoured City: new poets from Hull* (Bloodaxe Books, 1982).

Contents

'...which is a most parkely ground and Romancy pleasant place: heretofore all horrid and woody...'

JOHN AUBREY

'...the richness and extent of Yorkshire quite charmed me. Oh! what quarries for working in Gothic!'

HORACE WALPOLE

A Priest in the Sabbath Dawn
Addresses His Somnolent Mistress

Wake up, my heart, get out of bed
and put your scarlet shirt back on and leave,
for Sunday is coming down the chimney
with its feet in little socks,
and I need a space in which to write my sermon.
Although the hour's already late
it can still be done, if only you'll depart!
Down the pipe and out across the lawn
would take you to the station yard
in which you left your bicycle last week
and give me time to clothe in flesh the text
I have in mind for the instruction of my flock.
Please hurry, dear. The earliest note of the matin bell
has left its tower like an urgent dove
and is beating its way to woods outside the town.
The sun is up, the parish breakfasted,
the ghosts are all returned into the flint
yet still you lie here, shaming me with sleep.
Wake up, I say, for Sabbath legs
are landing in the grate. Go naked if you must
but grant me these few minutes with my pen
to write of how I cut myself while shaving.
Be useful, at least, and fetch my very razor,
for the faithful have set their feet upon the road
and are hurrying here with claims on the kind of story
which I cannot fittingly make from your sudden grin.

By the Fire

It's quiet here.
I'm dozing by a quiet fire
on a December afternoon.
I'm lying under an old coat
for the cure of my soul.
A recorder tune comes floating in,
and *float* is a good word.
It's vernacular,
just as the tune is charitable.
We go back a long way. We are old,
and need not listen to anything less.
There's a blend of arrogance and compassion
I've long been trying to put my finger on.
I think it lies beneath an overcoat too,
and hears the hiss of the gas,
and vagrant playground tunes.
When I close my eyes
I can still observe this room,
my table, the books, a milk bottle.
A bed of coals is glowing and dancing
in a grate that was torn out years ago
and it doesn't even seem strange.
I'm lying between two fires
in the quiet they've sometimes afforded me here.
I feel their warmth, and look —
my eyes are closed.

Truants

How long is it
since we fled across the fields?
We can't remember.
We camp in this broken railway house
or sleep in shallow ditches.
Butter floats in our black tea,
and painted pebbles dangle in our hair.

We do remember our predecessors though.
One, half-crazed, stayed away for three whole days,
almost too dumb to feel the cold,
afraid of the blame for a borrowed pushbike.
In the end policemen pokered his friends
with operatic frighteners that elicited his den.
They trembled. We trembled. The Majesty of Law.
There was laughter in the staffroom later
but mostly I think we envied him
his fear and his conviction, his adventure.
He turns an original face upon us now.
All that loyalty, he says,
all those ketchup sandwiches they brought me there.

The Bell

The Europe of the heart,
and a bright wood there.
Listen to the bell.
The ears attend
the spasms of a yellow bell.
Breath from its old mouth
subdues the quilt of countries,
a blanket on a sickbed.
The squares of mustard and the squares of potato
crumple under the heat,
which ruts like dogs
on the uninspected roads.
The hot wall of twelve o'clock
pushes history west.
Barns go down. Fields and churches fall.
The land permits
a hard tide of trees.
It is eaten by roots.
The heel of a gnarled hand
forges and bakes,
ferments and brews.
Ponderous and momentary hands
have twisted rope in rope-walks
and cast a bell in sand.
Someone was lost once.
Someone still stands immured
inside cold masonry,
exercising sound.
In the Europe of the heart,
in a bright wood there.
The yellow is like the flat of a blade.
The heat is from a chill belfry,
moving west with the trees.

Anatolian Sequence

1

going there on a
long train
like I did waking once,
the slate-eyed syntax
of the border
the way the left hand
door its window
and swaying connections
elucidate the mountain

2

whose god has erected
two signs
one on wood against
trespassing
and one perhaps on stone,
bearing the name
'Lake Van' it seems
in its signifier as
bottomless and deep,
a delivery
of the deepest
parcels of water

3

which are posted into
the space between
a man and a child,
who doubts the whole
demeanour
of this country
but look
it is, it is surely
getting more Turkish
cubing itself on glass
and steadily, greyly
announcing its profession

A Winter's Fancy

To write a Tristram Shandy *or a* Sentimental Journey *there is no way but to be Sterne; and Sternes are not turned out in bakers' batches.*

A winter's fancy.
I look out of my window
and perceive I am Laurence Sterne.
I am sitting in Shandy Hall.
It is raining.
I am inventing a Bag,
which will accommodate everything.
I'd weave it out of air if I could
but the rain slants down like a page of Greek
and the afternoon is a dish of mud,
far removed from gentle opinion.
I am heavy with God.
The weather used
to cloak itself in sentiment
but today it imitates the tongues of men
and wags in curtains at me, along a yard.
I am also John, an elderly bibliophile.
Once, long after I died, I returned to Coxwold
on a literary pilgrimage.
A red-faced lout leaned over my gate
and instructed me curtly to Sodding Sod Off.
He was full of choler.
I sometimes feel I can understand
what's been eluding me ever since Christmas.
I'm exhausting my karma of country parson
in a dozen lives of wit and kidneys,
caritas, the pox, and marbled endpapers.
Looking out from here, this afternoon,
I can just discern the porch of my church
where Nick and Numps are sheltering from
Thucydides, Books Six and Seven.
By the look of that cloud looming up like a skull
there will soon be nothing left to do
but to take to my bed.

The cattle squelch past beneath a sodden sky,
below my windows and before the eyes
of Peter Didsbury, in his 35th year.
I consider other inventions of mine,
which rise before me in the darkening pane.
Light me that candle, oh my clever hand,
for it is late, and I am admirably tired.

Traffic

A truck full of shingle
crawls past our window
on its way from the river

Its headlights are on

and it has the words
Ocean Derived Aggregates
printed on its side

I did not see this yellow truck
just heard you tell me of it

I was looking at the rain,
watching the water
bouncing off the pavement
and sluicing down the drains

Night Moves

'Workin' on mysteries, without any clues'
BOB SEGER

He got much younger and smaller.
Two police arrived and took him out of the bar.
The street received him as a child.
He broke away when he spied the fortunate bus.
I had to throw a handful of coins to him.
Shillings and dirhems clanged on the metal floor.
Our policemen frighten me a lot.
They weren't in any hurry anyway,
standing by the railings in the dark.
They still had hold of his friend.
Their car was parked in the side road
that leads to the Royal Infirmary.
The yellow doorway crawled along the kerb,
the kid in a jersey, the conductor with a moustache.
I stayed crouching for a long time
as if on a sunlit bowling green.
My open hand was filling with sodium glow.
The gaze of the police was like
the nearness of the pavement to my knees.
Night's inexplicable actions. These night moves.
The railings released the breath they'd been
holding on to all day.

The Smart Chair

I heard my own voice.
It came to me in a room and it sounded strange.
I didn't recognise it.
I didn't even know it had happened.
It was a dark voice. Or a very white one.
It was like your daughter when she said,
'Your chair looks smart', and then grinned at me.
My chair looked smart because it had a tie hanging over the back.
She's eleven years old, and although she knows I don't wear ties
she didn't know I'd been to a funeral, wearing that tie
which now improves my furniture. I wish I was able
to tell you all the things that filled the last two days
and which of them relate to that voice that came to me.
The wind in the brown pines on Church Island might have done,
and my fear when that truck moved over on the motorway,
because I really heard it,
but trying to tell you might stop me finding out,
and I've had to forbid myself enough already.
Certain proper names are forbidden to me now
for I will not have them do my work for me,
which ought to be done with a simple correctness.
It is like your daughter saying that the chair looked smart.
Just to make it perfectly right she put a knot in my tie
so that it was really being worn by the chair,
looped around the top bar of the back
and not just draped over it. I thought she did it with panache.
I thought this when I got back tonight after two days' travelling,
for of course I hadn't noticed at the time, and then I went away.
I slept in a white room on a striped mattress,
with stains that were like the maps of skerries and small islands.
Slept in darkness, naturally, not yet knowing anything
of the brown pines on the real island
or the attendant rocks for pegging Holy Sinners out upon.
This was all by the bye and for the morrow at the time,
like the stripes on the mattress, since I went to bed in the dark,
or like the poems by Reverdy and Desnos I got shewn after breakfast,
before our walk, before we started driving back,
before the wind that freshened throughout the morning,
moving the flowering currants that grew among the graves

and saturating with fine colour the walls of the houses that lined the coast,
turning them all into poets' houses, the houses of poets,
in which talk about seagulls was under weigh
in voices that had sometimes come to them in rooms this far from home,
rooms with white walls that sailed in old and natural darkness,
sisterly to other rooms in distant houses
with chairs and random mental furniture,
all living the same kind of life as pine-cones, gulls,
a cathedral wind in brown pines, old urine,
and faces passing backwards and forwards
on a narrow causeway with shingle and lapping waters…
from which I remember that I saw
that a white farmhouse stood in the middle of the bay
on a rock that was little larger than itself. *Not* a farmhouse,
unless they farmed seaweeds, rats, and the voices of drowned sailors –
there wasn't enough room – but just a white house,
a casa blanca to go with the gulf stream palms
and the bay tree on the cemetery island, a whitewashed house,
as surprising as the reflection of part of the name Lloyd
carried unruffled by the wind on the back of a black tombstone,
a mirror for its neighbour and as unsurprising
as if a high-backed chair had reared up instead,
instead of a white farmhouse in the middle of the waters,
a sentient chair, a really smart one, dressed in a black tie.

In the Glass

Pegs left out on the washing line
Catch the light of the moon.
They present a savage necklace
Which the night is taking off.
I look out over small gardens,
Like my mistress.
I see myself reflected
In the glass at the end of the yard.

The Surgery

Rose red rubble constitutes the evening.
A man with a worn and shiny billhook.
The coloured marble forecourts
Of shops that vanished in wartime.

In the waiting room a young girl and I
Smile at each other, are nice and shy together.
I count all the things that had something to do
With this branchy evening in the future,
The thudding of children on the old linoleum floor.

The Smoke

i can still smell the smoke

abandoning the upper case
for the first time in years
i (a little i)
sit in bed with
bonfires in my hair

if this poem is rather short
or if it is like it is
it's because i'm very tired
and i did not write it till tomorrow

Death of Pan

The wax ran down the trees in Tuscany
for each tree was a candle
and turned into features as it ran
for the candles were hamadryads
(a kind of girl) that melted as if on pyres

At Vallombrosa
the most Chinese place in Europe
we climbed through the pine trees and the cloud
to find that Milton had been there before us,
an Englishman,
who never heard the word "Tao"
though he'd stared into its cool and smouldering bowl

It's cold this morning and in the street
a scrawny female voice is heard, exclaiming
'the callous bugger'
to men who have been hammering nails in planks

The rowan is being stripped of its berries
from the top down, by starlings

The small still life on the chopping board
is nothing more than 'marvellous and empty',
a plastic flashlight half an onion
and a knife with its wooden handle bound in twine

Red Nights

The red industrial nights of summer
are typed on the back of a frightening letter,
one that will cause you an ongoing pain.
And tell you as little of the reasons why
as you'd expect from effete vernacular verses...
The word "soul", somehow set down right next to you
on the back step, freshened by a little light rain;
the way the south face of the chimney stacks
collects the light from the roadway going north;
the weathered blue fence that froze all winter,
nothing less than happy in its literary colour.
There are ways of deportment under skies that mimic fire
which I hesitate to commend to you at this hour,
which itself is only a fiction –
allowing the dawn a sudden swelling cold,
chopping like huge waters under a riverside pier.

Home Town

Children and dead sailors lounge in salty parks
or lie parcelled in oilskins in boarded-up shops.
He strolls among them with a sword
or finds himself alone by a grey and angry sea.
There is much to terrify in this seaside town.
A striding man from a medicine show
treads on the middle air and scowls at him.
A wind machine blows scraps of alphabets
which burn about his ears. He steps into an upper room
and the floor is no floor, but an idle bed of dangerous machinery.
He could have perished in those engines,
or fallen right through the house.
How does he always rescue himself? He does not.
Surely one of these escapades would suffice to encompass his death?
It would, but something always rescues him.
Dark children offer him their hands in parks
that bob against the street like barges against a wharf.
The drowned recline on their elbows
and smile at a bureaucratic mistake.
Perilous climbs bring him out of the theatre
and the wheels that should have burst him open
never get further than starting to turn.
What is beginning to frighten him most is the rescue,
not the predicament. If the charred ideograms would turn to rain
he could believe in it, but they simply cease to blow.
The vaudeville morgues are not consumed in a flame,
he just leaves them behind him on a drizzling quay.
The hand that pulls him from the cogs and gears
is not attached to an Angel but only to the dark in the doorway.
He parks his ancient Austin Seven on a steeply shelving beach
and leaves the handbrake off, for it will not plunge
into the tall unconscious waters but simply wait,
between the ocean and the town. He crunches shingle,
and wags his sword at the flapping bones of a winter resort.
His car stands patiently, with her head between her wheels.

Mappa Mundi
(for Alan Livingstone)

In their great houses there were always tables laid,
piled high with simple food and books,
old tables that lay supportive beneath
a drift of nutshells and paper, sharp tools.
Returned from walking behind the byre,
or spreading lant from casks upon the fields,
it was at these boards that they received
the urgent message from the capital,
pushing cheese and almanacks aside
to unroll the hasty map, slopping a harsh red wine
into bowls, spilling it, augmenting the stains.
Later, brooding idly and alone
upon required action they might scan
the worn incisements of their tutored days,
the musical notes whose deep square holes
enlaced a fertile cartography,
in which each emblematic creature rose
above a smoking town, and called aloud
to the beasts at the corners of the world.
It was cold, and there was all of Europe
to decide, and Europe, hooded like a bird,
blinked in its eye-gapes and shifted on its perch.
It was ice. The ink in its beechwood wells
snapped to the black attention of winter,
while fields lay supine in communion clothes
waiting for the word, and a coney limped
to the doorstep of the hall for warmth,
or just to perish there. Tables, shifted nearer
to the blaze, supported the elbows of men
who watched themselves in dreams, in the gases
vapours and *language* of the hearth, for they
etymologised, and watched for others too.
Logs of poplar's yellow wood, the splintered larch,
fed a conflagration which all men scanned
to know their mind or find their visitors:
still many hours away, for example, a grandee in furs
alights from his carriage at a crossroad in the hills
and knows he is regarded, as he bends

to fill the carcass of a fowl with snow,
as well as who regards him. His clear gaze
is lifted for a moment towards a house
he travels to but cannot see, then falls,
as the eyes of his host have also fallen,
back from this fire to an erudite table,
a table spread with the things of the world
and cut out from the local forest years ago.

Talking to David

Blue smoke rises how I envy,
goes silently where?
The slide projector's on,
and all the bits are rising.
Bedroom window focuses late Phoebus,
hot on cheeks and hair,
and another term is always somehow needed.
Researching candour with which to de-school ourselves
we look at Jesus plucking pigeons from the clay,
but it is looking in mirrors.
We fly over waters fifty metres deep,
the moats that encircle castles in Northumbria.

Country Alembic

On this tobacco convenient road two crows.
It is Vineyard Street, and they know they perch in it.

O my twa corbies,
that which is swallowed in our recursive ginnel
is that which is excreted.

December and January
wet their beds in Vineyard Street, wet their beds.
Drink your cigarettes,
and look up the road to the castle.

It's the 1500s again.
The rain augments the brown flood.

You sit in the car rolling cardboard into
Pharos of Alexandria shapes.
You wind down a window
and blow through them, open eyed, at the birds.

Scenes from a Long Sleep

i

He thought the Moral Code
was a pamphlet obtainable
(price 1/6)
from His Majesty's Stationery Office

If he ever got hold of a copy
he would read Mr Hore-Belisha's Foreword
while eating pies and pasties
in the Curious Angel, Glidington

ii

Cod and halibut basked on the waves
on the dark green Arctic main
One of them opened its fishy mouth
and delivered this quatrain

I can't go back to Greenland
They keep me out with an aluminium fence
It follows the coastline closely
I haven't used the Royal Bathroom since

iii

He stood in the window of his auntie's house
and watched the Great Apes
who were just invading the town

They came on their long arms,
swinging from the eaves of houses
and casting naughty glances at him

If he'd known the words
feudal, gable and *marzipan*
he could have fostered their employment

Instead he just stood there in his dressing gown
wondering how a straight street
could be turned into such a crooked one

iv

The orchards outside the walls are hung with fruit,
squares of green and gold that swaddle the stone.
We are looking at maps, my sister, both ancient and modern,
and this is how it appears to us, the usage of the land.
What a distance they walked, those two Royal Persons,
when they made their circuit of Byzantium.
I see them moving in gowns, stepping amid flowers,
siblings who have this city as their centre,
its noise and its heat a haze on their dexter hand.
I see them stopping to pull down fruit, now he, now she,
or passing through trees to cross the great roads silently.
The city is full of their commerce but the suburbs are empty.
I do not think they talk much to each other,
or know if much talk is necessary.
The light and heat are from a sun in his splendour.
It is, and will continue, the middle of the day.

The Guitar

Aerial songs, estuarial poetry.
An electric guitar is being played.
Its neck is five miles long,
and forms a margin of the River Humber,
where the thin soils are.
Aeolus swoops down, and begins to bounce on it.
He has serpents in his eyes.
He plucks the strings
with his Nebuchadnezzar toenails.
He's composing a piece called Early Memorials.
A train comes. His pinions take him
half a mile high in a lift.
The train courses over
the frets of the guitar,
but it is going backwards,
towards the hole in the middle.
Coleridge is sitting at a window
with his back towards the engine.
He must have been lunching in Goole,
but now he's fallen asleep.
'Dutch River,' he murmurs, 'Dutch River.'
He's dreaming of the advent of the railways
but will not remember, because I intend to
keep it from him.
It's a mercy that is available to me.
The train steams through fields of bright chives,
then it reverses and comes back as a diesel.
A madman steps out of a cabin and salutes it.
He stands by the flagpole outside his summer *kraal*.
The engine-driver waves.
The engine-driver and the madman
both went to the same school as me.
They sport the red blazer and the nose.

They chat for a bit while the engine grazes
on the chives that spring up through the ballast.
'Nice bit of road,' one says. 'Aye, nice road,' says the other.
The sky is like an entry in The Oxford English Dictionary.
The earliest reference for it is 1764,
in Randall's *Semi-Virgilian Husbandry*.
The loco swings its head from side to side
with the movements of an old-fashioned camera,
or a caterpillar. The mythic god of the winds, however,
who is still aloft, is getting tired of attending.
He flies up the line and starts twisting on the pegs.
Lunatic, driver, and diesel all look up.
Their faces assume an almost communal rictus.
They all jump in the carriage with Coleridge,
as the mighty lexicon twangs. They wish they were asleep.
The god puts his face right up to the window
and shakes his horrid locks at them.
They stare at the cattle grazing in his fields.
They note the herbaceous stubble
which makes frightful his visage of mud.

The Jar

His in-trays are everywhere, like the mouths of Avernus.
This month, my prayers have all gone down
through that jar on the hearth, whose green glass wall
collects intransigent air, and tells tales
of the life of the Buddha. Why complain?
The world will either school me with desires
or guard me with the language of madness,
I am promised my death, and the rest will
take care of itself. In the meantime,
those buddleia spikes are nodding sagely
like lovely Asian women, and an ant traverses
a gypsy clothespeg, fallen in the grass.
Although I grieve that the discursive mode
is lost to me behind swords of conjoined fire
I take the roads that open to other music.
The anguish of a single human soul
may flow into the world's receptacles,
jars, boots, boats, words, hollow logs and
emptied bottles of mineral water,
and therefore I invoke them all for my
Ode to Broken Thoughts – like broken biscuits,
shaken in a tin on an open hand
to tantalise as if we were children,
while that master grocer in a brown shop-coat
who postures as my psychopomp
looms up in the smoke of his language and virtues,
moustache and teeth and famous leg,
with his fawning theft of the wisdom of mothers,
and his tales of once serving the monarch, or God.

Part of the Rubric

Write out the word "picayunish" one thousand times. Make a solemn vow, never deliberately to discover its meaning. If the word is already known to you, ring British Rail on 0482 26033 and ask the price of a ticket to Edinburgh. If, knowing the word, you also live in Edinburgh, then go into the toilet with a hand-mirror and sit looking at yourself for precisely sixteen seconds. Write to me care of my publisher and confirm that you have followed these instructions. Please.

Eikon Basilike
(for the soul of William Cowper)

During the late and long continuing cold
I went for a walk in the empty heart of the city.
I stuffed the sun and moon in a deep string bag
and let them hang from my shoulder as I marched.
I noted the resemblance that my home now suddenly bore
to a level Baltic town, its frozen gardens, and its
bright green civic domes. The new white lawns
had frosted to such a depth that they'd lost
the visual texture of grass and begun to make pastiche
of a pavement, a complement to some old and
disgruntled buildings. I cast around for a route,
and chose to follow three hares in winter coats
who hopped across my path. They tempted me away
from that novel plaza which the ice revealed
and I found myself on a track beside a canal,
or rather a drain, which is different,
for it empties into the turbulent German Ocean.
There was dereliction on one side of the stream
and an Arctic kind of Xanadu on the other.
I shivered. My hip-flask was out of action.
I hadn't actually invented it yet
but knew I wouldn't be leaving it very much longer.
If this was what linguistic exercise meant
then I didn't think much of it. The deep structures
I could cope with, but the surface ones
were coming at me in Esperanto, and fragments of horrible Volapük.
I was walking through the urban fields that surrounded
the Stalag or temple or star-ship of the Power Station.
Yellow electricity vans kept cornering on the road
that crossed the bricky and entrenched landscape.
I recognised the faces of the drivers, and later spotted
most of the leading Romantic poets, all of whom were eating
substantial packing-up, in tents pegged out by the kerb.
It was a case of etcetera etcetera. Tiney, Puss and Bess
were proving considerate guides. I found I had plenty of time
to inspect the ceramic formers on their poles.
I noticed many ordinary things, several of which were lying
on the ice, between the high and weedy banks of the drain.

I began to think of the slicks of grey lawn that must exist
between runways on the edge of international airports.
Hot moonlit nights in Athens or Cairo, powdery channels of grass
that might just as well be anywhere, all of them rising in Hades.
The fat and impersonal transports were lifting on either side
and threatening my creatures with their cruel and silvery wings.
I could see the black pylons here and there but the power lines
were all of them lost in the low-level brume. I only heard them hum,
thrupping the atmospheric fridge with over and over again
a Vulgar Latin sentence which my guts were scarcely screwed to.
'It is all up with thee, thou hast already utterly perished.'
The hares bounded on, and finally halted outside the gate
on the bridge that carried the road across the stream
and into the precincts of the Generating Board.
I stood next to them, making the fourth in their row,
and I looked where they looked: below the rusty barbed wire
was an old white notice bearing the four bold letters
that denoted which mesmeric authority
we laboured under the caring aegis of.
Something – Something – G – B.
Like a name of God. But the letters were all wrong.
The three hares looked at me like animals in anthropomorphic films
when they've just led the hero to the scene of his triumph.
I thought I might begin to weep and yet I scarcely knew why.
The enamel plate was now announcing that this was *Eikon Basilike*,
a place whose sub-title I had no problem supplying
from my sad and emotional erudition, justified at last
by a portraicture of his sacred majestie, in his solitude and sufferings.

The Classical Farm

'vetus ara multo fumat odore'
HORACE, *Odes* III.18.

Flame in the evening windows of the school
has crumpled all the inside of the rooms.
Small fires smoke on every allotment below
but the source of the incandescence
is in the big red eyes of the Academy.
The kids have screwed hot sheets and planes of gas
to loosely fill the boxes of their absence,
have fuelled the massive antique stove of brick
beneath whose gaze the gardeners do their work.
An old man stands sagely folding polythene
and cuts it with a sharp blade from the east
which he reaches for without having to turn his head;
a golden bird aloft stands crowing into the cold,
and men who translate Horace in their sheds
are bending homewards, sniffing the air for rain.
All will come by wisdom on this spacious classical farm.
They stoop to pick up last year's brittle stalks
or clean a boot on a neighbour's crumbling fence.
They lean into the evening on their spades,
or calculate the autumns of each tenancy.
One has been here sixty years, a colonist
who wears his herbal fumes like cope and shawl,
another just a week, and both of them
are clearly to be reckoned in millennia.
The fertile grid behind me now includes
the altar, hearth, or small Vesuvius
of a cone I build and let the school ignite.
I am learning to know these fires, and have laid,
with funnel on top and a flue in its base to inspire,
my factory of ash for fattening small landscapes,
a working model of its great Platonic master.

The Pierhead

Slabs of water
slide on two rivers.
A dredger churns at the tide.
Its chains and hawser
make a brief stab at incandescence.
This is where
the Hull joins the Humber,
and the angle it draws
is just like the one on the map.
You can stand in it and gaze

at the last few teeth in a truly civic dentition, spaced along the bank. No radiance
like here. Compounded of bricks and water by the afternoon, it walks through door-
ways and helps to polish handrails and counters, scour wooden floors. It could put
a shine on bread. The sky has fooled with culinary metaphor. It's sharp salads in oil
today, a classic, almost tasteless dressing

which drenches walls and cobblestones like rain. The name of the goddess of arts
and trades is written on a board, painted in the livery of one of the old railway
companies. The windows of the pub beneath it stare at the empty shore a mile away,
at other windows, jugged with grey light. Mute and opposite hostelries wear faces
like slices of meat, haslet for example, and wait for Byron to swim between them,
for the ticket office is locked,

the last ferry has gone. A man sits perched on the roof of the covered pier. He's
helping to dismantle it, cutting through the girders with a torch. A white flame springs
from his wrists, and makes him look relaxed and critical, as if one more thing had
been done in his honour. He sits on the throat that used to swallow cars and cyclists,
rolls of lino, the wives and dogs of estuarial farms. The empty cross-section at the
fluvial end used to fill with the side of the ship, the paddle reversing in its semi-circular
house. Now it's just a frame to isolate some river with, an occasion to note the anguish
of fast waters, and to guess at the speed and volume of their flow.

The News

At nine o'clock tonight,
crossing the road to the off licence,
protracted crumps of artillery.
Not thunder,
finally here after weeks of dry weather,
and not the Fleet, either,
which is still off South America.
Probably drums and canisters,
demolishing some factory on the other
side of the river; or poems,
or other unstable munitions,
going off in a dump up in Heaven, or wherever.

The Rain

Text and Exposition of a Northern Creation Fragment, for Neil Astley

i

It was cold and mythological.
It was coming sideways,
out of wide leather buckets.
The cow looked miserable too.
They was usin' Norwegian Hats,
to scoop some scary, travelling
gallons at her...

ii

Lengwah oskoorah, como per stone-troll man.
Boskie, except no woulds or shoulds all that time,
but solarmente fake-its. Names like Linlithgow,
springin up like mushrooms, heavything in chaos
nd turnin into a cow. Spenz er time lickin
bark off this ole tree, she doo, likkin up Sol
n lettin it fizz on er tundra. Its Gertrude.
Bos by nomen Gertrude, meanin I of the day,
like Day's Eye, lickle yellow flower on lawns.
She have big sad rudes, roundels and mournful in them
all through the gert, and sumtimes by nighttime two.
It rains. As Dutchmen in their courage spraak
'Hit rayneth pijpestelen,' pipe-stems,
snapt clay rain with wholes ɸru the miggle,
witch brings us on to sound-change: deformed like miggle
R kekkle and bokkle, reseptickles for reign,
and manklepeace, but this need not be learned.
It is not in the Texas, and thus irreverent.
Sum phonemes diph-erunt in Niceland, esspeshly
for that old cow. Mudder milky and primal sacrud,
debutante in the larva feels all day
nd tryin to give berth to de world,
Adam nd Eve ploppin out de behine,
n muttrin in Shebrew, much as fallgoes:
Bearshit barrow elbow HIM,
ATE hash arm EYE him,
WE ATE all OUR ROOTS...

Nd as they mumble, their wordies tumble after,
big black let-us, like curly cow pats,
then claps of funder, mental fings
wot applord in the first drizmul doorning
of this nice planned-it Dehru. Lots of yellow.
All of them prattin about givin berf from their harmpicks etc.
Lots of fings sproutin in the shit and the butter,
a greenthyme beginnin ond ϕe brids layin eggs,
sky makin signs on the hide of wold Gertrude
and incest havin fun, like you can with six legs.
O noise! O-din! He oafens a Roger Casement
and show his crinkly cartoon smile. Dubbel ravings
are Disprin in his ears. They peck and bushel arownd his hed
like circumstandshall elegance, but dark. He pisses in his hat.
Udders will have yam for tea, or be *sic* in the bust,
but Gertie noo gats wazzed on by the god.
She fort he was upstairs, but parent-ly not.
It's coming at her sideways nd he's god all his frenzy with him.
Their faeces fill the side of the mounting, they luck as if
they're drunken lass at a nut-shy, they are like the hat,
they are fool of piss. Dilemma, waggin its horns.
Dingbat alone has the receptacle, the only deep chapeau
in the creole of asian yet, but wot about buckets?
Isseasy. When questings are arsed the gods will have the handswear.
The Dame has been droppin makars all this time, crawlin from every
nooky cranial, every horrorfiss. Poets and tanners,
nd tailors n perleasemen. *Flagrante*, her big mist-ache;
her Indus-tree and weird. It grieveth me, nd I try to look away.
A hat and buckets full of stale are blanchin-off the sky-signs.
I feel on her long tung the hot stale wot falls, I rôles her eyes,
but all the wile she is dropping trolls nd ice-men, she ignaws me.
She maketh boats of skin, nd pegs herself out for voidjiz.
She watches her killdren and attentive to their stories.
They are droppin kin from their nosethrills.
The mounting is several leaks away and all the yewrine
is comin this long trod on purposefull. It is coald.
More than Oding and his crew have throne by now,
she is mudder of ϕe whirled, and drooping that cum-panio
which turneth round n piss on her. It is loaf-weird. The weed-feels wave
and her kids go shod in shoon. She sees them fool the land
and their spoking languish dairify like farms. The bride seas
thrill with fish. The herows make death and marridges

44

and their lifes are whide nd green. There are slave-chains,
nd dryin fish, and pelts of gests on doors, nd choppin invitin
necks off, and outhouses, and wind, and buried standin up
neaf de doorstone of de byre, like wotsisname, Hrapp – hauntin the garth
nd lookin up the shirties of the girls, lookin for mudders,
all the white flints of the post-hole in front of him
and the daily reign of the homecumin caddle,
blockin the light from the crax in the pavement,
steppin across him, and bathin his north face nd hair...

Old Farms

Old farms
swallowed by town
remain as gateposts
brick paths
and sheds.

I'm walking through the graveyard
thinking about them.
I note how splendid
the local silage is,
and spot a hairy
half a coconut.

It's Caliban, the little monkey,
peeping out of the grass.

This life of intimations
amuses me.
We come from the oldest farms of all,
and eat our thoughts like apricots.

Glimpsed Among Trees

The house comes on line.
Information that streams from its eyes like dots
seeks out a person who kneels on a brown allotment,
the month being March and the time of day noon,
the long spongy root of a plantain grasped in one hand
and the sudden wide notice of the house's attention
conveyed in open assiduous envelope, down to this plot.
There is no moisture anywhere. Friable skin,
untouched since Autumn last, denies it.
A dry sheet covers the lumpy mattress
that aches in the scarcely visited bedroom,
the outside tap has stained its rags with rust.
A cold as square as furniture, but white,
not I, not thou, despite the urgency,
is emptying the old tradition
of the high gabled forehead lost among trees
and leaving a continuum behind.
Nothing whatever to do with the 'arid soul',
for it is not didactic, it makes the mind go blink
with novel gravities. The boy's room, revealed
as if in his absence, to the cleaner, by his toys,
shows the broken bowl of an eighteenth century clay
inverted as helm upon, and making to seem Mongolian,
the head of one of his metallic infantry. It snows.
His father the Doctor, demented by early hours,
leaves lemonade and cooking marsala
to go sticky in a glass, a tipple which
the blue-painted god of the morning absently retrieves
and carries with him to the topmost view in the house.
It is this broad prospect, and old 'intelligence',
which the kneeling man has knelt to cultivate,
and minutes spent replying to the sky
denote it well, the binary ons and offs sent back
up a still intact funicular to the roof, the line of the eye
engraved as in a diagram, Plate XXVIII for choice,
with barlets that pulse from a ball whose tender lids,
peeled back and gorgeous with lashes, will never blink
at that which is only physics, its trees relentlessly inverted
in air as thin as this and its cottages always held

behind hedges of optical glass, – it takes the petulant
volumes of lunchtime air to be libertine enough
to bring carelessness to empire, to bend that gull with fallacies,
or to plot the fog which will take the next day out,
a strike with a flannelled hammer to dispose
of sheds and cybernetic pastimes equally, which is what it does.
It turns the whole invective into neighbourly Walden Pond
with old and chimneyed Thoreaus standing round and hearkening
to the anserine cries in its reeds. It sinks the Marist Church
in a soup of such communion that its dedicated bell
can honour with one mouth the entire eroded coast.
Small flotillas hoot, the incoming geese give voice,
the larger cargoes stand in line off Spurn,
a white embankment indulges the Sabbath shore...It is the hour.
Noting the moon and the chains we are going to make our attempt.
We shall take this festering street and sail it home at last,
provisioned and coaled and silently observing
the estuarial forts as they slip by on the beam,
a drunken cry too close for the crew at the rail
and the Old Man biting his pipe and discerning,
'It is egregious, oftentimes. I lie in my bed
and wish I were mental, like Rawlings. I watch
the great timber of the plough, to which all the other
parts of the plough-tail are fixed, and I find that I am singing.
I say my prayers and do my certain sums. I like the number ten.
I am always counting on my fingers, or flexing my hidden toes
and I log those occurrences which I call my *Decades* daily.
Ten ivory beads in the form of geese breasting the air this morning,
ten sweet farts, ten persons of Belgian nationality, ten fascicles of tens.
I remember, once, I brushed against my sea-boots in the dark
and after I'd frightened myself incurred with growing joy
the thought of their emptiness as a witness to my work.
There are temples everywhere.' He ended,
and the problems of narration started up all over again.
That coathanger, hooked to the rusty guttering on the shed,
could not its suit of air be taken down and worn?
It is stitched with lights for the dance with the swart earth
and is only waiting for the dancer to come, whose coming was delayed.
Eighty years ago a girl out walking lost a button here
and it took down into the trench with it, sealed inside its glass,
the whole of the dusk which descended on the farm,
its fluting impermanent sounds, the language of the wildfowl on the drain,

the green and oily bulk of the engine, as it chained the evening
on its last and most festive traverse of the field. All this is known.
The button goes under the tap like a drunk, and its pitted face
is pinched between finger and thumb, and then pocketed.
Quartz from the lips of the tide shines like diamonds, then dies,
but this has been up and down in the earth, and has learned a thing.
Its stored reflections will always include the poles of the ferry at Hell,
its vibrations always be unwinding the band of the voice of the goose
as it beats from the drain to the dyke. I absolve you, oh my heart,
for you inhabit your vocative well, you have slept in old farms
and are watching the face in the glass, as Mr Lockwood did,
whose 'yell was not ideal'. Your only reader must absolve you,
for there is blood in your hand.
You have waked in the oaken closet of the day and found yourself kneeling,
the house overlooks you, and its phantoms regard you as real.

Cider Story

A daughter now for her blinded sire in England
Pronounces the Greek and Hebrew which she cannot understand,
Or carries him cider, along the whitewashed hall.

I hear her candid voice approaching, skirts on flagstones,
And it strikes me that, at twenty shillings a litre,
Cider is still, just about, affordable.

It is middle morning, one of those apple forenoons
Which make the fairest lineaments of England. I decide so
In my darkness, then return to my rigid black questions:

What kind of chair is this? Who released it from the native oak
With my person attached and set it down upon limestone?
The rhetorical pavement echoes the courteous step

Of my cool but resented dryad, who carries me cider,
Whose voice I detect in the apple-green light by the wall:
''Tis good for thee,' she comes trilling in consolation.
'And drink it up, now, that shall take thy mind off thy dole.'

A Shop

A small one in a seaport,
And a handful of semi-precious stones
Is rolling to a standstill
Along a cold tinned counter.
Light from the horn windows
Or which falls through greaseproof paper
Or which whispers words like "oilcloth"
Reveals in the never-startled gloom
The simple evil of its sallow owner
To the slowly swaying, and dull,
And indifferent, customer,
Who pulls the drawstrings on the curious skin bag
From which this realm of scattered islands fell
And pockets it, idly watching the hand
That reaches for the heavy octavo ledger
And rests a moment on its massive iron clasp.
Irregular jewels stud that burnished sea,
Each garnet and carbuncle circumscribed
With three concentric lines, as on a map.
You are witnessing the typifying transaction
Of the commerce on a planet without redemption,
Where unredeemed adventures come to rest,
As somewhere they must, in the borrowed trappings
Of time and place, example and occasion:
A den near a harbour on a late afternoon
On a distant sphere where the fog and the bells
On the doors of the shops on the islands like dark gems
Conspire to evince a permanency of winter
I doubt if I am licensed to portray,
And which causes me to end these verses simply,
With what, when that large book is opened,
I pray it may contain, which is itself a prayer.

On the Green Phone

(for one whose Muse had departed, from another in the same predicament)

Ah yes, that emerald telephone
On which you ring me up to say
That the world of objects is empty.
Once it would have told you stories
On nights like this, but now it copies
The heart, and rings and then goes dead.

It's the same with me, old friend.
Some bastard somewhere with all the luck
Has written a poem which features a cloud,
A scarf, a lettuce, and Lithuania.
I confess because it isn't me
That I'm glad it wasn't you,

Allowing us both in charity to concede
All power to his elbow. As long, of course,
As it wasn't *him*. I couldn't stand it.
He wouldn't know his bum from *Locksley Hall*
Where *all* the rooms have derelict
Green handsets, and coils of bindweed

Are confusing the exchange. 'Don't worry, Boss',
We've been through this before – at first,
Each time a poem got laid to bed
Herself would throw a wobbly, if you recall,
And now, when our first books are published,
She's out the door again, her *Coriandre*

Corrosive in the wardrobe, and lipsticked insults
Drying on the glass. 'No need to fret',
But that's the point, you have to.
It's the scratching that shows the wound is healing
And at least when she left she didn't take
The inwit needed to describe the symptoms.

I once had a friend who, when he heard
Phones ring in unattended booths,
Would answer as the Indian High Commission,
Or God, or whatever took his fancy:
'I am the ghost of Howard's grandpa;
This is the voice of the lettuce you ate…'

It almost provides a model for both
The Muse and her subscribers, who
Are often on the line, occasionally answered,
But mostly observing the long hypnotic brrr
Of the dialling tone's unusable dimeters,
Or sometimes misled by a passing lunatic.

I've said enough. The hour is late
And the charges too prohibitive for us
Properly to pull these metaphors together.
Like you, I think, I apprehend the irony
Of kind remarks which assume that the girl
Is still in residence, or, even worse,

The unkind ones with which her recent absence
Would tempt me to concur. It's hard.
For myself, I'm putting my faith in history,
And the sudden fact that I tell you something
I dare not tell myself – 'She'll be back,
The green phone will ring again
And the furniture be swelled with fictions,
Like the heart. Convince yourself of that.'

White

Waking at seven
to thick white fog

a candle still burning,
the stereo unit
still receiving power.

Window open –
good old boy,
for floating me in
and out all night,

not much birdsong
dark tree-shapes
one or two pigeons
pretending to be telephones

A Flyte of Fancy

When I die and arrive at the Pearly Gates
I shall doubtless discover
that Saint Peter is poorly and taking a few days off,
and that David Harsent has been booked in his saintly place,
who does not like my poetry.

Saint Peter would have asked me about rain,
knowing the thing I used to love behind all,
but David Harsent will insist upon discussing
pustules, catheters, feminine endings,
underpants and schizophrenia.

Among the things that make this poem a bad one,
and one that Harsent will be *entitled* to dislike,
is the specialised knowledge it assumes on the part of the reader.
The name of God's friend is known to the quick and the dead,
but who in the world has heard of David Harsent?

A Man of Letters Recalls an Incident in His Youth

I met him in the early morning hours.
I'd said goodbye to my girl and was walking
Back through the slanting streets to my lodgings.
He limped. A bullet wound. Small calibre.
And certainly the cloth was torn and stained.
He told me a story I could do nothing to but attend,
And must have asked directions to a hostel
For he ended up on my floor that night, though I
Recall that I offered my bed. Having me down as civil,
Privileged, I do not think he could understand
That third-floor room in impoverished Paradise Square:
The one-bar fire, the empty soup cans,
The ewer and basin composed on a marble slab,
The ridiculous chintzy chaise-longue. Neither could I.
He had a baffled interest in my dignity, but he was mute,
Reminded me of other toughs I'd met. One, in Soho,
Who wanted something with my name upon it
Before he'd cash a desperate cheque, was scandalised
When I showed him a summons from the Dean of my College.
Was that *good*, or had I been in trouble?
He needed something he could judge me by
Outside my presence, neutral, in his Blue Room, Adult, Cinema Club.
He sounded like my father; and I confess I have been pleased
With an interest that approximates to love to find
Most of these persons naïve beyond belief.
This one had quitted the City in the morning,
For his health, was going North with his story.
I seem to remember he would not accept any food,
No tomato soup, just a cup of coffee and an aspirin
Before he stretched his damaged leg to sleep. I lay in the dark,
While his snoring settled down into a rhythm
Acceptable to the alert piazza outside. Familiarities.
Night-birds cried in the slum of the rectory garden.
The switch on the meter revolved, the fire died with a clank.
A metal bucket beneath the laden desk
Waited for one or another young gentleman
To empty its contents over the landlord's bike,
Which stood chained to the apprehensive railings,
Directly under my window. I think I froze.

I began to consider my girl again, and then to writhe,
In a kind of pensiveness, stifling my rigid breath
With gulps, in case he would awake. What guest was this,
Who might be feigning sleep? I asked myself a question
That was answered by my shame. It didn't matter.
Just a criminal, who might rob or kill or disapprove of me.
A man whose story I half believed then forgot, and certainly one
Who would have a lot of pain from those stairs the next morning.

Long Distance

When last I called you up long distance
I thought the peculiar noises you made
Were caused by your sucking the flesh of crabs
From legs and claws in a dish by the phone,

Whereas what you were really doing, you told me,
And which I find just as pleasing to imagine,
Was licking Guinness-froth from your fingers,
Having just been out to buy yourself a bottle.

Events at the Poles

A metal shack in Antarctica,
home to several military personnel.
Another one like it near the North Pole,
this time full of meteorologists.
They look quite cosy, with their yellow arc-lamps,
their chimneys smoke away in concert
as if they both drew fire from Vulcan's caves.
All is silent. The equinox approaches.
Up to the door of each of the cabins
there trudges a postman, bearing an Easter egg.
The soldiers greet their caller gladly
and take him inside for a cup of cheerful soup.
The weathermen, though, who are all very surly,
can think of nothing else but the coming dawn.
They sign for the egg and send him on his way.
For some time afterwards his stumbling black dot
provides the major visible difference
between the two landscapes, then suddenly he's gone.
Nothing moves at the white ends of the earth
except two similar columns of rising smoke.
There's nothing to distinguish them for a minute,
but then a door like one on a furnace opens
and out steps a postman, turning his collar up.

The Hailstone

Standing under the greengrocer's awning
in the kind of rain we used to call a cloudburst,
getting home later with a single hailstone in my hair.
Ambition would have us die in thunderstorms
like Jung and Mahler. Five minutes now,
for all our sad and elemental loves.

A woman sheltering inside the shop
had a frightened dog,
which she didn't want us to touch.
It had something to do with class,
and the ownership of fear. Broken ceramic lightning
was ripping open the stitching in the sky.
The rain was "siling" down,
the kind that comes bouncing back off the pavement,
heavy milk from the ancient skins
being poured through the primitive strainer.
Someone could have done us in flat colours,
formal and observant, all on one plane,
you and me outside and the grocer and the lady
behind the gunmetal glass, gazing out over our shoulders.
I can see the weave of the paper behind the smeared reflections,
some of the colour lifting as we started a sudden dash home.
We ran by the post office and I thought, 'It is all still true,
a wooden drawer is full of postal orders, it is raining,
mothers and children are standing in their windows,
I am running through the rain past a shop which sells wool,
you take home fruit and veg in bags of brown paper,
we are getting wet, it is raining.'
                                    It was like being back
in the reign of George the Sixth, the kind of small town
which still lies stacked in the back of old storerooms in schools,
where plural roof and elf expect to get very wet
and the beasts deserve their nouns of congregation
as much as the postmistress, spinster, her title.
I imagine those boroughs as intimate with rain,
their ability to call on sentient functional downpours
for any picnic or trip to the German Butcher's
one sign of a usable language getting used,

make of this what you will. The rain has moved on,
and half a moon in a darkening blue sky
silvers the shrinking puddles in the road:
moon that emptied the post office and grocer's,
moon old kettle of rain and idiolect,
the moon the sump of the aproned pluvial towns,
cut moon as half a hailstone in the hair.

Eirenicon

These old blue boards
Were once a part of the fence.
Now they form a side
Of the much neglected compost heap.
They warrant a couple of lines
In a hopeless libretto of courtesy.
The night is full
Of such embarrassed recipients.
An iron pail,
Blanched in historical cement,
Mimics the cough of a child.
Simple poems,
In the gift of the summer,
Get shorter,
Deconstructing themselves.

The British Museum

We dream of the British Museum.
We want to return a winged stone lion
To the desert country it came from,
Outside of which it is dumb,
Outside of which a stranger to meaning.
The plaque that rests on its foot tells lies.
We know this script that decorates its flanks
And it does not mean what the keepers would assert.
They have built a vulgar café in an annexe
Which seems to feature sexual machines, vibrating beds,
For lunchtime liaisons we're supposed to think of as cultural,
But we won't. We're busy dreaming ourselves political.
An elegant system of sleep is constructing
A complex lodge for a free and scholarly people.
A state of grace that lies sleeping within the State
Is emptying its present halls of plunder.

The Globe
(for Leo Doyle)

Men are not gods. They just hold the same things in common.
Climbing the stairs to our bedrooms in the dark,
or idly gazing at landscapes from early albums,
crouched in a plastered outhouse of a summer evening
where it's cool and quiet and the light has failed,
we harvest the truth of those tentative statements
which were formed in the mouth of the bakelite wireless,
for its plummy plurals have continued to reach us
wherever we are in the house. Edifying Lectures at Dusk
float in and out of the windows like paper planes,
the kind whose bombload is held to resemble
the light reflected from jams in the pantry,
pear halves stacked in syrup in jars,
the breath of apples in the air raid shelter
and the sound of the clock in the hall that is ticking like fruit.
Please ask me nothing. A globe of inky but translucent glass
is slowly inventing itself, and turning into a sky.
The yellow panes of a window expand upon it and curve
like four birds flying away from a centre.
I stoop to look through them at mountain lawns
and a bent old child with a barrow on a path
who gradually straightens and shrinks, while I do so myself.
There are bird baths on Olympus, too.
Dressed in gas masks and a good deal shorter
we are playing French cricket next to one,
passing the bats around and around our legs
and eyeing the prizes of perfect fruit it supports
as if the centrifuge on the end of the arm
had just created loganberries and now sustained them.
The garden levels as I watch; the fence comes upright with a click;
a sigh from the bellows of an unseen camera –
and the outspread palm of the evening is holding up the house.
Here. Its bootscrapers stand in little religious alcoves
and vie with the kitchen drains in collecting the dark.
The bells in the bedrooms are stopped with paint
as fast as the mouths of the days of its servants.
A towel rail hums in the bathroom, a stirrup pump stares,
a medical dictionary sighs on its shelf,

and trolley bus tickets with different owners
flutter like moths in the back room we shared,
just glimpsed, as I open the door with love
to gaze at the absent inmates on the grass,
flying back to their piles on the dressing table,
and alighting in serial silence, like the days.

What Care We Shew

What care we shew, when we answer those who are sleeping.
Replying to questions about pits and burning towers
we utilise a grave and kindly voice.
Old heraldic hands, couped at the wrist,
clasp in the air beneath an ornate lintel.
The words are formed in different rooms of the dark.

The Barn

I stopped in the barn's wide entrance,
where the dust and chaff were like bees.
With the light behind me, and my rake across my shoulder,
I knew I resembled the Harvest as often portrayed.

"Bees" is what we used to call
all kinds of insects then,
and bees were in my mind as I crossed
the floor to where he'd fallen.

I'd never known him dead before
and therefore did not see him straightaway
but thought he was a sack,
with a barrow standing nearby ready to move him.

And move him I did,
though first I stood on that earthen floor
for a hundred years, while the language changed around me.
Dust. Chaff. The names of common things.
My hand moving up to touch my tightening cheeks,
to pick the pieces of broken bees from them.

The Fly
(for Ian Curtis)

Legs finer than this hair that just fell
it alights on my block of white paper.
I was going to write something down
but now I must pause to watch it work its feelers.

If even the otter is more different than it seemed,
'reacting simply to the sound of running water',
carefully plastering cruel loudspeakers
with sticks and mud, what can I say of this fly?

It has legs. It has antennae. It will have a triple-
jointed Latin name. Trying to get a pupil once
to describe inventively an inhabitant of Mars
I broached the subject of its sense-perceptors.

I wanted him to imagine a better way
of eating than punching a futuristic machine,
don't ask me why, was hoping he'd require
that it gulp phlogiston with its cerebral limbs,

extract subtility, or at least employ them
to carry its clearly audacious food
to the mouth on the top of its head. Blank stares.
The dutiful teacher must sometimes be content

to consolidate vocabulary. 'Look,' I said,
and put the backs of my wrists to my brow,
like a Spanish child playing bulls. 'What are these?'
And waved my fingers around, intent on eliciting

the strange questing life of our benevolent alien,
the skipping ropes that started from out the dome
which housed his spirit and his intellect. *Ex ducere*.
By art I would "draw out" that which he did not

know he knew, something known before to which
he'd give the word, and justify my salary. 'Quick.
Come on now.' He looked at me as I just looked
at that fly which landed on my empty paper

and lovely recognition dawned, with all its expertise.
He put his fingers to his temples, waved them round,
and snatched his hesitant answer from the air:
   'My Martian, when he eats,' he said,
     could use his, you know, testicles.'

Vesperal

spiders, lately,
warm dry days,
and spiders everywhere

we'd probably call this
"spider autumn"
if we kept that kind of calendar

tonight you brought one down in a shoebox
and I put it outside
and then just sat and listened to the house

faint airs moving
across the mouth of the chimney,
our old white fridge
turning on and off in the dark

The Mountain Hare
(for Mike Boyd)

A white mountain hare
sits quietly on a stool
and watches the curatorial evening
fall through a bottle of wine.

Stuffed in 1926, you know
it has nothing left to fear,
has nothing to do but embody the silence
and share the light from the river with the walls.

It tends to be like that in this Museum,
and since such events are hardly other than real
the hare has decreed that henceforth they'll be known,
for simplicity, as December Afternoon.

Everything here, says the mountain hare,
resolves itself into aspects of collection:
while careless tides ascend the nearby staithes
some Sky drops in, to take a look at our bones.

The Northlands

No rain. No storm or thunder,
not even on the wireless. No lightning,
no rain.

But I'd been watching the lightning!
Either bounced off local cloud
or reflected in lucid mesmeric radio
from over the horizon
three whole days now,
which nobody else had,
and for three whole days I'd
thought I had epilepsy.

Not until I heard some tune
I hadn't been listening to
and which didn't impress me
was a Chopin nocturne
and saw how it and the night sustained each other
like two old con men telling each other tales
did I actually get the point,
and the intimate cruelty,
of the day's imitations:

a casual spread of laundry in the bath – Ophelia;
creased and mottled leaves from Summer
on Susan's Miss Moffat cap – the cunning Butterfly;
myself with fountain pen in hand,
– ah how much better than history.

Which is why
I'm confessing from here it was from here the first time round
that the lies *really* began and I began to imagine
the hills with all their electrics stilled
and *cattle pinned out like photofits in the glare*
and *my house that laughed in a curtain of rain*
but didn't embarrass me, though it should have done,
and even…
if I'd died that night how it wouldn't have meant
quitting this kingdom of metaphor

but leaping off the body fag in hand
to be some new kind of god for the northlands,
the *northlands*,
which actually frighten me,
which far from being a place
are a set of sounds whose transcription I think
it would be unwise to leave unrepented for very long,
whose transcription thank God
I think I am *unable*
to leave unrepented very long.

The Sleepers

They lie on short grass,
in a place where whiteness
builds hedges to filter the blue,
nowhere more than a dozen yards away.

Time eludes them.
Passing clouds have stained their backs
with unfelt shadow,
but otherwise nothing has moved.

Their small enclosure is the perfect frame
for all that a lengthy posture can express
of love or of strangeness,
two hands of cards disposed by careful hands
face down upon the turf,
as if in the expectation of return.

Hare's Run

Hare ran on mountain,
disclosed the boundless accidental
graces of his running.

What he did was go on up at speed,
consuming the functions of visibility.

He went in flame,
with feet of flame went utterly beyond.

A circular town of grey volcanic stone
when hare had passed it
unfolded into a bright assembly
the petals of its story,
its doorways and herds on an incandescent wind
were drawn by hare up the mountain.

For as fast as hare but always just behind him
his curious consort stepped
and glanced into caves where practitioners of breath
returned his stare from sudden columns of ash.

And still hare travelled upward,
and sprang across the tightest of the lawns
until the leprous slabs asleep on the summit
which now will bear his clover prints for ever
allowed him to lift through the towering stacks
of charcoaled birds his final narrative form.

Hare vanished then.
His shadow raged an hour among the rocks
and then went cold and died.
Of the thousand stories about him now in fashion
there are those which make urgent claims on hare's behalf
and those which simply invite the listener to tremble.
A while after hare had made his run on the mountain
a hissing rain commenced.
A few of God's more willed and habitual stars
arose unseen behind hare-shaped windows in Heaven.

Gillan Spring

What I'm about to write
has a necessary premiss:
I'm lying on the ground
in a kind of ancient encampment,
scrubby clearing, skin tents, stockade of thorns.
I can't raise my head for some reason,
perhaps because I'm pegged out with drying thongs,
so most of what I see and can report
is feet, sometimes bare and sometimes shod,
in bark or hide, is legs and the
clothing of legs, wound round with strips
or lost in the circular weight of a turning skirt.
The people here seem gentle enough,
so perhaps there is rather a wall of hanging vapour
which only leaves a yard of transparent air
like the breathable space near the floor in a burning house
and I'm lying down to feed my eyes in it.
Maybe it's the curtain of time,
which is usually taken to be vertical
but might well be horizontal, a blanket really,
and the wind has lifted it up for me to look.
However this is, there are certain things I can see
it would be wasteful of me not to try and relate,
the feet I've mentioned, but also the contours
of the bases of various heaps of equipment and
material, the fan of smallest bones
that have fallen from that large bleached stockpile
or the butts of the lances of ash
arranged in their careful tripods near each lodge.
Much of what I said earlier is extrapolated from this
and some of it calls on the language of geometry,
like the trapezium made by two legs planted apart
and crossed by the parallel lines of the ground and the fog.
It is through these early windows, so to speak,
that I gain my largest fragments of the camp,
the way the land drops away to the south through the scrub
and the sheen of distant water, mesmerised with birds.
There are poignant moments too. A stream of urine
arcs down from a hand that grasps its fleshy tube

and one of their small women, squatting to piss,
looks directly at me, with the only eyes I have seen,
for the body that crumpled fell with its face in the earth
and the most of the business has taken legs for its text.
It is as if I am at leisure, prone in the door of a tent.
My cheek collects the spattering drops of spring,
or there is sunshine, which is beauty, or snow,
which is a beauteous darkening, the way that wood
and skin and bone go black in a world of two colours,
when the working floors are covered and the wisest
people die. There is necessary laughter.
To some things, though, I cannot ascribe a season;
the doors of blood are perennial. Between two pairs of legs
that move a shouldered pole across my screen
depends the head of a stag going backwards,
its throat wide open and its antlers inscribing the dust.
With her feet in the hand of a boy, for I see him
as far as his chest, a swan prolongs her crimson neck
between two ruined fires, and a third
which it seems is never extinguished, for its hearthstones
are blackened with eld, and its topmost flames
are necessarily lost. Art, I am told,
concerns itself with the difficult and the good,
and this I'm inclined to believe. Not far from here,
no more than twenty minutes away by car,
is a field I first discovered in mid-winter,
its fringe of trees and scrub, its ponds,
and its permanent spring of clear matutinal water.

The Best Translations

A man invited a demon into his house.
That is the whole of a fairy story,
the familiar kind of popular horror
which lies below each classical literature.

The tale is made of an upstairs room
a civil square a casement and her shoes.
The best translations are those which had him
flee the temple in anachronistic clothes.

A Monastery in Georgia
after an account by Alexander Elchaninov

He climbs all day to get there,
ravine going down on his left.
Two stone towers,
two black "beards",
water a mile away.

The bread is mildewed. They eat it in
the sunlight that visits the terrace.
The young one hems his robe,
the old one limps.
He was thrown from the wall last winter
by bandits who gained entry and found Nothing.

Twin towers. Two black beards
which wrestle with the liturgy.
He sleeps under sheepskins in his cell.
He walks in the pines and meets two men.
He only has two words of their language.

The nights are memorable.
The window embrasure is empty
except for the cold spring lights of the town,
where his mother sits, and his sister plays the piano,
where his hands rinse photographic plates
beneath the moonlit tap in the kitchen. He turns.

He snuffs the Georgian sky and then the candle.
The icon goes out, and I take my pen
and borrow his simple story of long ago.

Men have lived. Even so far from us
in place and time as this. John and Gregory.
I speak their names. I record my joy
that I did not have to invent them.

The Restoration

Birthday candles, strewn like the spokes
of sadly dismantled wheels,
could be screened going backwards,
could be seen to go back on the cake.

And brutal clowns, from their half-way down the lane,
could by invisible hawsers be recalled
to mend the innocent carts the very
sight of which had caused them to go berserk.

There could be restored, in the cinemas of time,
the luminous frames we imagine preceded the action,
even from splinters of wood and ruined foods,
the many morsels of glistening bright *gâteaux*.